NO VILE THING

ALSO BY BRAD DAVIS

Short List of Wonders
(Winner, 2005 Sunken Garden Poetry Contest)

Though War Break Out
(Book One of *Opening King David*)

Song of the Drunkards
(Book Two of *Opening King David*)

NO VILE THING

Books Three & Four of

Opening King David

Poems by

Brad Davis

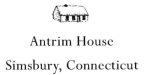

Antrim House

Simsbury, Connecticut

Copyright © 2008
by Brad Davis

Except for short selections reprinted for purposes of
book review, all reproduction rights are reserved.
Requests for permission to replicate should
be addressed to the publisher.

Library of Congress Cataloging-in-Publication Data

Davis, Brad, 1952-
No vile thing : poems / by Brad Davis. – 1st ed.
p. cm. – (Opening King David ; bk. 3-4)
Includes bibliographical references.
ISBN 978-0-9792226-9-6 (alk. paper)
1. Bible. O.T. Psalms–Poetry. 2. Religious poetry, American. I. Title.

PS3604.A95558N62 2008
811'.6--dc22
2007046501

Printed & bound by United Graphics, Inc.

First edition, 2008

The cover image is a detail from from an engraving
by Barry Moser, "David in the Valley of Elah."
(For the full print, see page 3.)

Author photo: Bill Pratt

Antrim House
860.217.0023
AntrimHouse@comcast.net
www.AntrimHouseBooks.com
P.O. Box 111, Tariffville, CT 06081

For those who struggle

ACKNOWLEDGEMENTS

The following have published a few of the poems in this collection, and I am indeed grateful:

City Works: "The Good Life According to *Architectural Digest*"

Connecticut Review: "Genuine Replications"

Hill-Stead Museum: "After a Snowfall," "Better Far," "Genuine Replications," "Glory," "Insomniac's Commission," "Less is More," "Short List of Wonders, Besides that Summer Sunrise from the Train in North Dakota: Sky, Horizon, Prairie," "Sing for Joy" (all from *Short List of Wonders*, winner of the 2005 Sunken Garden Poetry Competition, judged by Dick Allen).

My gratitude extends as well to friend and first critical reader Robert Cording; editor Rennie McQuilkin; Pomfret School colleague Kathe Atwood who, as the library director, provided me with an office in the library where I completed work on this book; and Deb Davis, wife of thirty-some years and final critical reader.

TABLE OF CONTENTS

BOOK THREE

BOOK FOUR

NO VILE THING

BOOK III

When I tried to understand all this, it was oppressive to me.
Psalm 73:16

OFF JAKE'S PIER

— Fish Point, Maine

North through the square, gull-stained arch:
lobster boats, terns, cormorants, osprey – the whole
confetti-strewn harbor – and above the far rocks
a stunning new "camp," senatorial among more
representative habitations. Been a few harsh words
among longtime locals – Jake, one of them –
resenting inelegantly how the camp's
casual grandeur alters the scale of the entire bay
and renders more and more obvious their own
homes' dull and sagging lines. Yet all this –
the point, the harbor, the new camp – inheres
from one moment to the next so perfectly
not one atom in the retina of a seal pup ever goes
suddenly missing. Why, it almost seems we are living
into a prefab universe rising immediately beneath
and around us. But more likely nothing exists
even five minutes from now, and we, along with all
things, are figures in an inscrutable *poema*
that in each instant of becoming is not here, here,
then gone like a phrase in a jazz improvisation
sustained seamlessly over the architecture we call *time*,
and only by what we call *mind* do we grasp the immense
beauty – and terror – of its coming in and going out.

Turn your steps toward these everlasting ruins.
Psalm 74:3

North Housatonic

Two decades back the state cleaned up the river.
Now, with innumerable swallows sweeping
this way and that above her light rapids,

I wade along the rocky western edge
and nod to the week's last fishermen and day-
tripping paddlers in their rented canoes.

It is good to be on holiday in Connecticut,
isn't it? No longer at odds with how we came
by this real estate – loving our mail-order

hats, wide-brimmed and draped with
mosquito netting – the late afternoon hillside
awash in the fast fade of something like alpenglow.

No one from the east or the west or from the desert
can exalt a man.　　　Psalm 75:6

To Exalt Oneself (Quietly)

i.　　　Dismiss as insufficient
　　　the egalitarian nod of sunlight;

ii.　　　With one hand,
　　　set in motion all machinery
　　　as may elevate the self
　　　above the muddle of one's peers;

iii.　　　When this works, feign humility, and

iv.　　　With the other hand,
　　　engage the protocol
　　　for irreversible advancement
　　　into your pantheon of choice;

v.　　　When that works, retire,
　　　gracefully

vi.　　　Disappear, averting your gaze,
　　　lest anyone beneath you see your eyes.

He is feared by the kings of the earth.
Psalm 76:12

ENOUGH

In a garden, one word, and a new way bursts
open in the redneck heart of a fisherman:

an old accessory of war falls, dropped
beside a severed ear, and God in the mayhem

stoops to take up again not the sword
but the ear and attend to the wounded.

Ever since God told Abraham
that He is not a deity who desires the death

of a child, the change was in the works.
And now here, in a garden,

with one word God reconstitutes
the modus operandi of his people on earth;

in an instant, blood-weariness blossoms
into rebuke – *Enough!* – and to make example

to the strong and weak, the brave and bitter
of this world, God lays down his arms.

I cried out to God for help; my soul refused to be comforted.
Psalm 77:1-2

OPENING DAY

Classes at the school where I work begin on Friday.
The newly renovated student union will teem

with teens buying books, playing air hockey, snacking
on burgers and fries from The Tuck.

A far cry from School No. 1, Beslan, North Ossetia
where last week, armed with guns, bombs,

and a short list of demands, pro-Chechen militants –
male and female Allah created them – secured

the campus – one thousand students, teachers, parents
assembled for convocation – and captured

headlines everywhere – 300 dead, 700 wounded – a bold
stroke rendering frivolous the evil I plot in my bed at night.

Yet if I despair of either my fullness or their
affliction, then I succumb to what I know is a lie

but cannot name. This claims my heart: the scores
of school children fleeing through broken windows,

their captors' bullets finding them mid-flight, silencing
the light, filling up the sufferings of Christ.

I will open my mouth in parables.
Psalm 78:2

JUBILATE

Praise the parable – the story it tells – and
how it means and
what on earth it may mean and

the way we, like children, keep returning
from our well-meaning forays, ever circling back
to the broad lap of this thing or that for what may sustain us.

Praise how we keep arriving at point B
having begun typically at some point A, the wonder
of otherness being the new wine that makes our heads spin.

Beware the closed circularity of the disenchanted,
the *a priori* rule that refuses any chance
of an intersecting transcendent. Such a rule is

no rule recognizable to the story itself but
only to those whose long and short days – round and round and
round they go – will end in futility or worse.

There is a story that is not this poem that this poem
tells nothing of, except it is a parable well worth telling and
to know it makes a difference impossible to overstate.

May the groans of the prisoners come before you.
Psalm 79:11

LESS IS MORE

Am I the only one, sick of news
from Jerusalem, to wish the land

would vanish, all belligerents with it?
Perhaps a tear in the time-space curtain,

then — *whoosh!* — gone — West Bank, Dome
of the Rock; from the Golan Heights

to the Gaza Strip — all of it instantly
sucked off stage, removed like a wart

from a thumb, a thumb from a hand. Trust me,
I dislike collateral damage as much

as the next guy, but how long these headlines,
the inhumanity, daily mirror

of perhaps my own insufferable heart?
Here, founded on similar sand,

this house of loathing lies pitched toward
a fall that would be my future

were I to anchor myself inside its walls.
How I wish it, too, would meet with

irreversible deletion: a start to the end
of all wars against the blessedness of innocence.

"Of Asaph. A psalm."
Psalm 80

E-MAILS TO ASAPH

1.

My take on what you presented in class?
Great refrain: the intimate, even fearsome

desire named by parallel verbs aching
for satisfaction – to see the face of God –

and in that moment of the poem, three times,
nothing else matters, not form or content.

2.

Sorry the class's feedback felt unfriendly,
but your peers had the good of your "psalm"

in mind, and in the end, as I said then,
its final shape is wholly up to you.

3.

Yes, I reread the poem. Closely.
Another strong point,

given the supplicatory nature
of your piece: consistency of person.

Unlike many of David's psalms
that flip from first to second to third then

back to first, this one of yours
sits well, first to last,

in the second person. That said,
look again at your opening six lines

and reconsider Nicole's comment
about mixed metaphors.

4.

Fine.

If your God's good with mixed metaphors,
who am I to argue.

But for future reference:
just because you hear the poem

as a song lyric doesn't excuse you
from having to deal with issues of craft.

P.S. Drop/add ends Friday.

Begin the music, strike the tambourine.
Psalm 81:2

SING FOR JOY

Which is not as immediate as, say, supper
or as titillating as chicks or fame,
but in a sad world where, no matter how well
we eat or fuck or preen, all things
tend toward suffering and diminishment,
maybe there's nothing better to sing for
than such joy as may buoy us up,
return us to a "right mind."
Provided there is something to rise or
return to, without which we face, at best, a long
and inconsequential fiction
with no possible happy ending,
no hope of reinstatement,
no royal lover of souls to take us back.
Broken and bitter as we are,
if we cannot sing for joy, why sing?
To show how clever we can be? How much
better than trees at making meaningless noise?

You are "gods"— you are all sons of the Most High.
Psalm 82:6

In the Humanities Library

*— A man can receive only what is given
him from heaven.*   John 3:27

After hours, he shares workspace
with a housekeeper's radio audible

throughout the building's modern,
multi-level foyer. It is tuned in

to a local station: soft rock, weather,
news, the occasional talk show.

He shares it also with a card-sized copy
of a Russian icon – the Savior's gilded

Descent into Hell – image
of the crazy hope that he keeps

for now on his chair's wide arm.
The housekeeper's name is Virginia.

His office door opens onto her domain.
Daily – he is never present for it –

she dusts, vacuums, empties
his trash and recycling, the job

both gift and embarrassment,
and no matter how she repositions

his papers — *every piece in its pile,*
every pile in its place — he never

feels piqued, only grateful, as when,
seeing him enter and begin the climb

to his third-floor cell, she turns down
the radio's volume. A bit, anyway.

Enough certainly for him to hear
and receive the difference.

O God, do not keep silent.
Psalm 83:1

EVEN A POSTCARD

Like, say, one of those
stupid ones with a fat couple
eating massive ice cream sundaes
on a park bench at some beach
and a rude caption like *The Bigger
The Better* on a curly blue banner
splayed across their lumpy shins,
but no, not even that. So what
was I supposed to think, you
on that Greek island all summer,
I behind the express cash register
at the same old supermarket, and
up walks your twin sister all smiles,
her cart loaded with low-carb
salt-n-vinegar soy crisps and lite
beer; so yes, her party sounded
pretty damn happening, and yes,
okay, her lips are softer than yours,
but what the hell did you expect?
That I'd get all religious about
our love, become some kind of monk
for you? Think postcard. Even one
stupid postcard.

My heart and my flesh cry out for the living God.
Psalm 84:2

BETTER FAR

I am a speck lodged in the hem of a garment,
dust in the tight weave of a fabric draped

sari-like around the divinity-beyond-imagining
whose nature limits his wardrobe to what is

of love and lovely beyond whatever we may mean
by *beautiful.* Suspended here, I am ecstatic.

Though cancer and suicide have taken friends
and former students, and ideologues everywhere

stain the air with their maniacal raving,
not a day passes without my grateful amazement

that I have not been swept from my small place
by some fastidious hand that knows a hitch-

hiking piece of lint from an integral thread.
Better far this hour than never to have been.

Faithfulness springs forth from the earth.
Psalm 85:11

GLORY

Seems the ground knows when to begin –
October, October – pulling on the dark

dugs of this good forest, and year to year
you and I, bundled against the chilling air,

draw close to hear the suckling and smell
the sweet milk of wet, fallen leaves.

Consider the earth, and think faithfulness –
a tilted planet rounding its solar course.

This year our steps are slower, our hearts
distracted by a flooded basement apartment,

a goddaughter's recovery from a coma.
So we promise ourselves: next October

we will get outside more, attend more fully
to the woodland's face flush with self-offering.

Among the gods there is none like you.
Psalm 86:8

HERE, NOW

I wish
the indistinct voices

across this lobby
were charged with amazement

at the miracle of being.
What harm would it do?

And that,
listening, they heard this rain's infinite

polyrhythms as metaphor
of an infinite delight

in a universe of infinite particulars.
What possible harm?

The Lord will write in the register, "This one was born in Zion."
Psalm 87:6

HUNGER

When they laughed – junior highs
packed in a lockered hallway,
fisted snow flying like blown kisses –
they looked at each other
as though nothing in the world
could possibly separate them: the first
circle I ever wanted into.
Then there was that soccer team.
Then those quiet painters in art class
whose work shook my bones loose. Then
the shaggy six in long wool coats who smoked
hashish, wrote poems, and made by hand
their underground magazine;
like a stray pup desperate for a pack,
I would make their seventh.
Which is simply to want a place, a chair
in the circle and not be a fraud.
This would be hell: to want
and want, like an unignited wick,
and die wanting, an old dog at the door
and no one home, the house
abandoned.

I am set apart with the dead.
Psalm 88:5

MY SPIRITUAL PRACTICE

When I sit still in my office for ten minutes,
the lights turn themselves off. I love being

overlooked first by the lights' motion sensors,
then by those who assume I would not choose

to sit alone in a darkened room. They pass by
looking for me elsewhere. I do not care

to be seen by anyone. I am never tempted to wave
an arm and trip the affirmational switch.

Invisibility suits me. I enjoy imagining others
deciding I must be out sick or on an errand

or that I finally delivered on my threat: to buy
a one-way bus ticket anywhere south and west

of this office in this suburban private school
where, several times a day, I make the lights go out.

Who in the skies above can compare
with the Lord? — Psalm 89:6

LAST SUNDAY IN PENTECOST

A broad shadow angles
　　across the back field —
　　　　proprietary buzzard

　　sweeping bare treetops.

I thrive in late November.
　　Though wars and rumors
　　　　of wars and all things

　　turn from bad to worse —

this: a warm, clear morning,
　　the breeze and sunlight
　　　　practically Caribbean,

　　the bird shadow, pelican.

BOOK IV

All our days pass away under your wrath.
Psalm 90:9

THE GOOD LIFE ACCORDING TO
ARCHITECTURAL DIGEST

In a tall, open-walled poolside pagoda,
    suspended from teak rafters smooth as marble,
        saffron curtains like festal banners descend

in waves from a sweeping, hand-carved canopy
    that once topped a Buddhist temple in Thailand.
        So much for reverence in south Florida.

Some days I want out of this modern mishmash,
    this hang-loose apotheosis of the au courant.
        But where to go? The same

irreverence travels with me, clings to my every
    move like Spanish moss in the live oaks surrounding
        the redeployed pagoda, and I want

that poolhouse, pool, those lawns and live oaks,
    the uniformed staff of twenty-five smiling Cubans
        who minister like spirits to the elect of God.

O, I know splendid when I see it, which is why
    I never turn down certain invitations, nor
        will I ever allow my subscription to expire.

You will tread upon the lion and the cobra.
Psalm 91:13

ALISON

Their daughter, twenty-three — a depth charge —
does not like to be "fucked with" by insurance agents,

the media, presidents in pinstripes who, like sub-
marines running deep, assume they are safe

from the shallow grievances of ordinary citizens.
But she is not afraid of dying well, of descending

through the halflight with her weighted payload.
A lover of poetry and the lyrics of Radiohead,

none of her favorite verses make any sense,
though she can recite them from memory

as if they were nursery rhymes or quotations
from Chairman Mao. On the morning she explodes —

this is not a question of if but when, the world
unwilling to defer to her grand ambition for justice —

their nonsense will be on her lips the way prayer
will be on mine. The difference between us:

she longs to behold the suffering of the wicked.
More and more, I have no desire that any should perish.

My horn shalt thou exalt like the horn of an unicorn.
Psalm 92:10

VISITING BROOKLYN

I dreamt of flying low above a herd
of unicorns moving rapidly through a tight,
deciduous forest. That morning when I shared
the dream with my son, he asked — ever
the audiophile — "Did their hooves thunder?"
All I remember: not one animal was white
and horse-like, but closer to the ground,
razorbacked, with broad hips and shoulders;
their fabled horns were not the slender shafts
of medieval tapestry but rounded protuberances
of yellow bone; and I somehow understood
my welfare rested on staying with the quick-
turning herd, hardly knowing what this means:
Lord, exalt his horn like that of a unicorn.

The world is firmly established; it cannot be moved.
Psalm 93:1

A Christmas Poem

– for Roy

The surgeon did not plan on nicking
your carotid artery or spending
the holiday contemplating suicide.
The last report I received from Judy,
wife of your cousin Paul: the next
seventy-two hours are critical.
Will you wake from your coma alert
or something less than yourself?
You have two daughters – will they
grow up not knowing you? Judy said
that your family is big into God
and you are an elder in the church.
Then you understand, no doubt, how
your sudden condition, the simple
effect of accident, has an incisive way
of disturbing the theological peace
of those who are comfortable in Zion.
The Lord reigns. Yes. True. But
this happens, and now you lie there,
as lively as a lawn in December.
Me, I'm itching for a few easy answers.
Like "God is love." Or "This, too,
is your path." Or "The Lord giveth,

the Lord taketh away; blessed be…"
Galled and itching to lay waste all such
comfort as may be neatly swaddled
in the hasty brocade of piety. Sadness
is the province we inhabit: tundra,
endless cloud cover, precious little light.

"My foot is slipping."
Psalm 94:18

GENUINE REPLICATIONS

The pitch in the subject line being for neither
pharmaceuticals nor porn but watches,
this morning I decided to open the SPAM.
Good news: the watches are not those fake
knock-offs any tourist can pick up cheap
on a big-city sidewalk, but honest-to-goodness
replicas, authentic pieces of jewelry that cost
a tad more, but you know what you're paying for:
peace of mind, that feeling you know and trust.
Language is not the enemy here any more
than industry is the enemy or government.
When I consider the immense and terrible
perfection of a class-five hurricane, the purity
of a tsunami, or a quark's thrilling song and dance,
I do not comprehend how anything perverse
ever could have evolved anywhere in the universe.
That you and I exist at all makes no sense:
from primal forces dumb as the chair I sit on
rises sentient personality? Not likely.
And not just sentient but snivelling and self-
absorbed, arrogant and pathologically cruel.
Explain this: I feel ashamed of my own kind.
Some humans are even bored, determined,
it would seem, to prove that they are also stupid.

On some mornings it is easier to believe
nonsense will resolve into meaning and God
will pay the wicked what they deserve.
But this is not one of those mornings.

In his hand are all the corners of the earth.
Psalm 95:4

A Winter Sea

Bill's camera rests in my lap.
He is walking alone up the beach he and Donna

would visit each New Year's Day.
The wind is cold. There is no snow.

This is the first anniversary of her death.
He has asked me not to take a picture of him among

the dozen or so couples out for a stroll.
I snap a few shots of a white horse and rider stopped

before a shoeless girl on tiptoe, nose to nose
with the steaming mare. The little girl must be freezing.

When the day's prints return from the lab,
I hope he will forgive me.

Worship the Lord in the beauty of holiness.
Psalm 96:12

WHAT HOLDS US BACK

The Lord reigns —
> *let the earth be glad —*
>> and Sunday to Sunday says

it's about a body: mind-
> house, love-pump, engine
>> of desire. Was he or was he not

human? Did he or did he not
> rise from death? Sunday
>> to Sunday, if about nothing

else, then: a body's flesh,
> blood, bones, veins, teeth,
>> the whole vast prairie of nerves,

topography of parts, seemly
> and unseemly. Was he
>> or was he not all that we are

and more? Beyond merely
> good, his earth-gift, being
>> for the body — yours, mine —

declares our bodies good
        beyond imagining, and how
                we receive it says whether

a body, having died
        and changed to be like
                his body, passes on from this

thinning coil to that thief-
        thick Paradise where he
                has gone before and now is.

*

What holds us back:
        the foolish things we do
                in the body, always in the body

yielding to lust or anger,
        the gravities of unbelief.
                Even the least foolish thing.

The mountains melt like wax before the Lord of
all the earth.   Psalm 97:5

You Are Goliath

The stone is flying at your head,
and if you cannot dodge quickly enough
or deflect it with a brain pulse,
what's the harm in yelling, *Become bread?*
This may make no difference
to the stone, but what if – flash – and
it's a tiny loaf that hits you like an edible
doll pillow, and okay, the thump
to your noggin makes you blink,
but there's no pain, no blood,
and recovering instantly, you notice
across the way a kid's jaw drop – the aim
had been perfect – slack as the sling
in his hand, and you realize that stories
can have unexpected endings.
Whole histories can turn on a word.
And you smile slightly the moment before –
did you doubt that your enemy
could prevail against you? –
a smooth, well-aimed stone crashes
against the high wall of your forehead.

He has done marvelous things.
Psalm 98:1

AFTER A SNOWFALL

Above a shapeless field, the fine, up-swept tip of a redtail's wing.
On an unplowed road, euphoria at spotting it suddenly.
Then later over tea, delight in recalling the moment's perfection.
And now this.
                    If all were mere necessity, then why such beauty?
We are perhaps the only witness to what we think we see
and long to enter – a sacred grove, a new earth, a father's well-
prepared welcome home – and so leave behind all want, all sorrow
for what never fails to spoil our truest effort.
                                        My wish:
to hold close the wide, miraculous world I lumber through
shouting, *There!* and *Over here!* or waving subtly whenever
words or sudden motion might send it fleeing – everywhere rejoicing.

Worship at his holy mountain.
Psalm 99:9

The Oblation

– Blackcombe, BC

Delivered by chairlift, surrounded
by sundeck and sitting at a walnut-
stained picnic table, I had come
for the rugged, rock-peaked horizon
of the Coastal Range – and now
these ten centimeters of overnight snow.
Did I say it was July? And yet
what snuck up and claimed my attention?
A black she-bear who lumbered
into the clearing just below the summit cafe,
her snout probing the slope's rough-cut
grasses and low shrubs for anything edible.
It is one thing to approach large nature
telescopically, quite another
to have large nature take an interest
in your cheeze nachos.
I had re-read the tourist's wildlife guide
and listened closely to the day-hike staffer
review the likelihood of encounter:
what to do if.... when.... Hey, I'm good
with possibilities that lack a pulse
or body temperature, the hypothetical carnivore

that hasn't dirty claws or yellow teeth;
when you consider her
there's nothing categorical in her eyes.
But what looked up at my nachos, at me, then
back at my nachos was neither hypothetical
nor some toothless stunt bear in a carnival sideshow.
And as she rose on her hind quarters
for a better look at my six dollar snack,
I felt the universe, in a calm, subsonic whisper,
invite my participation in the practice
of nonattachment. Never
more motivated to be spiritual,
I lifted slowly the flimsy white paper bowl out
over the edge of the sundeck — a deal
is a deal — and tipped it, releasing a clumped
wad of corn chips into thin, mountaintop air.

We are the sheep of his pasture.
Psalm 100:3

In the Right Direction

There is shouting, and then there's shouting
for joy. I don't believe, having grown up

a card-carrying member of the library caste –
"quiet society" – that I have ever done either, though

the day that editor said yes to my Thanksgiving rewrite
I yelped and sank my teeth ram-like into my wife's derriere.

I will have nothing to do with evil.
Psalm 101:4

No Vile Thing

At a sister boarding school, lice: body, head,
and pubis. One rich girl's dreads infested,

they estimated, with maybe two thousand
resilient nits per natty lock. Her daddy had her

driven to a clinic where, once shorn and shaved,
they dipped her, so I heard, in malathion.

Though inconvenient and socially embarrassing,
it is not difficult to delouse a human body.

Foul surfaces, too, can be scraped, scoured, white-
washed, stripped, bleached, repainted. There's hope

for soulless things, nothing a little money
and cleverness can't cook up to restore a right

appearance for whatever has lost its sheen.
But what of those who long for more

than just a reclamation of unseemly exteriors?
For, say, the ripping of envy from a heart

or for such love as is quick to take measures
sufficient to cure a soul? The girl's body

will return to a dorm room made new, the clean form
return to function. And what then? What bath

to restore the good dream: such high regard
for all things, all people, that we may see God?

You sit enthroned forever.
Psalm 102:12

INSOMNIAC'S COMMISSION

One desert owl among ruins, alone
on a housetop – it is my job

to take this census of what remains
since the bombing stopped.

If I had been able to sleep,
if I had not taken a walk through town,

I never would have known
she was there, her cries, her dark

profile beautiful above
the silence of this god-awful place of dust

and wind-scattered ashes.
In the morning, I will fold up camp,

file my ridiculous report,
move on to the next empty village.

All my inmost being, praise his holy name.
Psalm 103:1

DIRECT ADDRESS

Odd the way King David spoke to himself –
Praise the Lord, O my soul – in the imperative,

the way he spoke to angels and the works
of God's hands – *Praise the Lord, you his angels*

and all his works everywhere – as if, without
his speaking it, they would not join the chorus.

Ah, conviction! Yet address one's self, one's soul?
In the popular sense of the word, wholly

schizo: David speaking, so it seems, across
some deep, internal divide or through, say,

a locked door, and I'm not sure who's inside –
the soul or the speaker – and who is out

or whether David's soul ever spoke back,
told him, in the imperative, to *shut up* or *bug off.*

The birds of the air nest by the waters.
Psalm 104:12

MORNING

Clothed in light, stripped
to creative will and wisdom's

unerring eye for detail, he looks
over the earth — wind and aspen,

eagle and prairie, river
and wild horse — and, like a bride,

she trembles under his gaze.
In the early chapters, we are

henna on her slender neck
and ankles, a string of pearls

between her breasts, a gold
thread slung low across her wide

hips and belly. No reason yet
to wonder at our being here.

To you I will give the land.
Psalm 105:11

Short List of Wonders, besides that Summer Sunrise from the Train in North Dakota: Sky, Horizon, Prairie

In a winter-flattened wheat field, the hundred or so
wild turkeys I mistook, at first glance, for geese.

Facing east, the sky in Connecticut half-hour past
sunset – an infinite cobalt glaze, a pearl-gray moon.

This desire: for grace upon ridiculous grace to lighten
the solitary heart of my one child now grown up.

And this, too: the inscrutable furnace that warms
my rooms, her iron pipes fussing endlessly over nothing.

They exchanged their Glory for an image of a bull.
Psalm 106:20

MANIFESTO

Restore a good thirty pounds, wash off the make-up,
put a bullet in the punk brain of the boyfriend
who plies her with heroin, and the sad woman
nodding at the café table next to ours might be
pretty, able to do more than – let me guess –
play the pouting starlet in his internet videos,
the green room confection at his crappy gigs.
How to bring an end to all that is tawdry,
release to the captives of the lie, the needle,
the culture that has high-handedly thrown off
the truth of original nobility, the image we bear?
I want to ring down a razor-sharp curtain
on all who profit from easy mockery or the cool
separation of beauty and meaning. So let us
with imagination – with films, plays, dances,
photographs, paintings – subvert, on each one
of its well-funded campuses, the University of Pornea.
I want a good future for the sad, skinny addict
that her idiot boyfriend cannot begin to comprehend.

NOTES

Epigraphs and biblical quotations are borrowed/adapted chiefly from the New International Version of the Bible, with occasional glances at the King James Version and the 1928 *Book of Common Prayer*.

Page 13 *(Psalm 73):* The word "poema" (suggesting "masterpiece") is lifted from the New Testament letter to the Ephesians (2:10) where it refers directly to the community of those for whom it was written ("we are God's *poema*") and indirectly to all humanity. The inclusion of "all things" in this charitable estimation is in step with the primordial vision articulated in *Genesis 1-2:* "God saw all that he had made, and it was very good."

Page 16 *(Psalm 76):* At the arrest of Jesus, his protective sidekick Peter lopped off a man's ear with a short sword *(Luke 22:47-51)*. Nice sentiment, bad move. This poem attempts a thematic linking of two very different biblical narratives: one calling off a hideous ritual (Abraham's sacrifice of Isaac in *Genesis 22);* the other calling off a last-ditch effort to prevent a hideous ritual (Peter's defense of Jesus who, within twenty-four hours, would die on a Roman cross). Both stories seem to say that, when feeling out of control, we humans should avoid resorting to blood-violence against one another, regardless of what culture, nature, or resolute moral reasoning may dictate. Certainly this would be consistent with the love of neighbor and enemy preached by Jesus.

Page 17 *(Psalm 77):* "filling up the sufferings of Christ" (see *Colossians 1:24)*. It is a disturbing prospect that, until his sufferings have topped out at some inscrutable measure of fullness, human suffering must continue. (Do I misunderstand?) Elsewhere St. Paul puts this idea (or one similar to it) into a larger perspective: such suffering, combined with becoming like Jesus in his death, contributes to the glorious prospect of resurrection from the dead (see *Philippians 3:10-11)*. Though not easy to warm up to, this vision, if we are willing to believe it, aims at helping us make positive sense of our suffering.

Page 23 *(Psalm 81):* The concept of "right mind" is a Buddhist virtue and also refers to the state of mind (and soul and spirit) to which a demoniac named Legion was restored following his healing by Jesus *(Luke 8:26-39).*

Page 32 *(Psalm 89):* Jesus regards "wars and rumors of wars" as part of the normal historical context preceding "the end" when "the Son of Man comes in the clouds with great power and glory" *(Mark 13).* Of them he says, "Do not be alarmed" (verse 7). The pelican is a traditional symbol for Christ.

Page 36 *(Psalm 91):* The final couplet attempts a contrast between the Bible's old *(Psalm 91:8)* and new order *(2 Peter 3:9)* attitudes toward the enemies of God's good purposes.

Page 37 *(Psalm 92):* "unicorn." It is peculiar that the King James Version translates the Hebrew *reem* as "unicorn." The NIV has "wild ox."

Page 38 *(Psalm 93):* The phrase "comfortable in Zion" is borrowed from the prophet Amos *(Amos 6:1 ff.)* who railed against those who claimed to be all about God but who, absorbed with the business of maintaining their comfortable lives, neglected the poor. "The Lord reigns" is the opening declaration in *Psalm 93.* The other quotations are from *1 John 4:16,* pop-religious culture, and *Job 1:21,* each of which has been often misused as a springboard to the denial or devaluation of genuine struggle and suffering. The poem participates in the biblical tradition of lamentation (e.g., the entire Old Testament book called *Lamentations* and, in the New Testament, *Matthew 5:4, Luke 19:41, John 11:32-36* and *16:19-22)* wherein grief is deep and fully felt yet not without a glimmer of the Hope that finally, against all pessimism, will not disappoint.

Page 40 *(Psalm 94):* The notion of "pay back" (cf. *Psalm 94:1-2, 23)* connects with the eschatological expectation that, come the Day of the Lord, the haughty oppressor will be brought low and the humble oppressed will be exalted *(Luke 1:46-55).*

Page 42 *(Psalm 95):* The white horse and rider were not invented for the poem; they were there that day. The little girl, on the other hand, may not have been; I don't remember. She may simply have become necessary as the poem developed (pardon the pun). In the "nose-to-nose" moment of the poem, I have sensed a conflation of biblical images: the mounted, conquering Messiah in *Revelation 19:11* ff. and all creation, personified in the little girl, thrilling at the arrival of the long expected Jesus *(Romans 8:18-25)*. Certainly Donna lived and died in this hope.

Page 43 *(Psalm 96):* The opening quotation is drawn from the poem's triggering verses *(Psalm 96:10-11)*. The debate over the bodily resurrection of Jesus is not an invention of modern scholarship; the apostle Paul, in his first letter to the Corinthians, dedicates considerable ink and parchment space to the controversy (Chapter 15) and concludes that if the body of Jesus was not raised as the gospels declare, the entire Christian thing collapses utterly and "believers" are fools most to be pitied. Granted, the resurrection metaphor, free from any controlling historical necessity, still has a measure of affecting power, yet this deliteralized sense of the word (reduced, in effect, to a rough synonym for rebirth) reflects a philosophical reticence toward affirming that it was the power of God that resurrected – changed and raised from death – the material body of Jesus into a spiritual body that now both enjoys recognizable continuity with his material body and transcends it. In modern ears, resurrection is a thoroughly outlandish concept. Then again, the resurrection of Jesus may very well have been the single most outlandish event in human history. Of course, so much depends on who one thinks he was; consider *John 1:1-14, Colossians 1:15* ff., and *Hebrews 1:3*. Could it be? Finally, "thief-thick Paradise" alludes to Jesus' conversation with the criminal who died on a cross alongside his *(Luke 23:32-43)*.

Page 45 *(Psalm 97):* The David and Goliath story is found in *1 Samuel 17*. This is, for me as an early 21st Century American, a profoundly political poem.

Page 46 *(Psalm 98):* "a father's well-prepared welcome home" refers to a parable in Luke's gospel (15:11-24). That which "never fails to spoil our truest effort" is human sinfulness *(1 John 1:8-9)*.

Page 47 *(Psalm 99):* The concept of "nonattachment" is a Buddhist ideal that has a Christian analog: *Luke 12:13-31.*

Page 50 *(Psalm 101):* "What bath...?" This is not some veiled allusion to the practice of baptism. Baptism is an act of radical identification, inclusion, and hope that anticipates an inner cleansing but does not effect it. Two beatitudes of Jesus come to mind: "Blessed are those who hunger and thirst for righteousness" and "Blessed are the pure in heart," for the hungry will be filled and the pure will see God *(Matthew 5:6, 8).*

Page 52 *(Psalm 102):* The owl and the ashes are images borrowed from the poem's triggering verses *(Psalm 102:6 and 9,* respectively). In the poem, the owl has become an emblem of the divine presence in the least likely of environs.

Page 53 *(Psalm 103):* The quotations in this poem are drawn from the psalm, verses 1 and 20-22 respectively.

Page 54 *(Psalm 104):* Reading this psalm of delight in the manifold works of God, I enjoyed a moment's feel for how, before the fall (thus, in the early chapters of *Genesis),* all things, all creatures, and humanity existed peaceably in the perfect pleasure of the creator, the earth being "like a bride," humanity like adornments selected for the bridegroom's delight.

Page 55 *(Psalm 105):* Though in the spirit of *Psalm 104,* this poem was launched by the phrase in *Psalm 105* that reads, "Remember the wonders he has done." Whereas the psalmist takes forty-plus verses to recall a few of God's wonders, my "short list" requires only four verses, five including the title. And, yes, human desire and the good things that desire hath wrought are among the wonders of God's handiwork and participate in his grand *poema.*

Page 56 *(Psalm 106):* The phrase "the image we bear" is from *Genesis 1:26-31,* and *"pornea"* (impurity) is anything that works against the grain of God's *poema* and the "good future" *(Jeremiah 29:11)* God intends for humanity and all creation.

About the Author

Brad Davis is a lecturer at the College of the Holy Cross in Worcester, Massachusetts, and edits the *Broken Bridge Review* at Pomfret School in Pomfret, Connecticut. Winner of an AWP Intro Journal Award and the 2005 Sunken Garden Poetry Prize, he has had work in such journals as *Poetry, The Paris Review, Michigan Quarterly Review, Tar River, Double-Take, Puerto del Sol, Ascent, and Image*. He is the author of a chapbook, *Short List of Wonders* (Hill-Stead Museum: 2005), and of two full-length poetry collections, *Though War Break Out* (2005) and *Song of the Drunkards* (2007). These and the present volume are the first three works in a four-book series entitled *Opening King David*. Brad Davis is married to a jazz vocalist, and they have a married son who is a musician and recording engineer in Brooklyn, New York.

COLOPHON

This book has been set in Perpetua, designer Eric Gill's most
celebrated typeface. The clean, chiseled look of the
font recalls its creator's stonecutting work.

To order additional copies of
NO VILE THING
or other Antrim House titles
contact the publisher at

Antrim House
P.O. Box 111
Tariffville, CT 06081
860-217-0023
www.AntrimHouseBooks.com
AntrimHouse@comcast.net

For discussion topics and writing suggestions, as well as additional
notes, biography, images, and work by Antrim House poets,
visit the Seminar Room of the Antrim House website:
www.AntrimHouseBooks.com/seminar.